# STUCK

## A POET IS A WORLD, TRAPPED IN A POEM.

AARCHI ADVANI SAINI

# Contents

# Contents

# Contents

# Contents

# Preface

If you ever fall in love with a writer, please run away. as if you stay, oh, darling if you stay, every utterance, every action, every blunder, every memory, every grief, every tear, every lesson, every word, every scar, will always be remembered, and never, ever, neglected. if you stay, you will soon be struggling with yourself in the middle of the night, as that's all we are good at, messing things up. that's all we will ever be good at, annihilating things, and then grieving over the heartbreak, letting us drown in the ocean of memories.

tell us one wrong thing and we will keep on nurturing that with the same love that we bleed on our poems. we will succumb to depression, tell ourselves we deserve this pain, convince ourselves that this is the only kind of love we have ever known, the kind that blows you like a storm, not the kind that will settle you down.

so, if you ever fall in love with a writer, please pack your bags. and run the f*ck away!

ps: don't date a writer. :')

# Aarchi Advani Saini.!

Aarchi Advani Saini

[ ] Author of the book "The Loads Of Poetry"

[ ] Social media "Aarchi Advani Saini"

[ ] Aries, believe in destiny.

[ ] Author of the book "The Loads Of Poetry Part One and Two", "The Journey of Love", "The Way to Love", "The Anonymous", "Let's be Confidante", "New Self", "Error", "The Cabalistic Child ", "Confession", "Dark Dead", "Half Dead", "Faith is All", "Anjaan Ajnabi", "Lifeless Life", and more.

Aarchi was born in India in 25$^{th}$ March 2002, the daughter of Sanjeev Advani Saini and his wife Mamta Saini.

AARCHI ADVANI SAINI.!

Author

She becomes one of the youngest author of her hometown Shamli. For this Danik Jagran newspaper covers this news, Later, many news channels interviewed her. So renowned for "The loads of poetry). She has sold the book worldwide, the recipient of numerous prestigious awards in her writing journey. She writes daily columns syndicated throughout the world. Aarchi Advani is well known for her writing on many other platforms. She is also a fantasy and literary fiction author specializing in "Life", as well as her upcoming book "Dream".

She publish her 10th book as her Hindi novel called "papa".

She also hosts a channel where she uses her passion for storytelling. And a background in business to help other creatives navigate their writing. So she is compiling an anthology named, "Of Your Choice", And her publishing journey is another level, she is good at her writing skills, but no one knows how to write books, same with her, but with the passage of time, she grows. When she's not writing or tubing she enjoys listening to books,

Making stories on her own. And love to live in her virtual world.

# 1. Day '1'

"Little things"
It didn't take much to make her happy. A gentle breeze out of nowhere that waved her silken locks, a little kid selling flowers at traffic lights, a group of sparrows feeding on crumbs at the terrace....

There was something about the way she smiled, that made the world seem a little brighter. It didn't take much to make her happy. A gentle breeze out of nowhere, a little kid selling soft toys at traffic lights, a group of sparrows feeding on crumbs at the terrace, just some random babies on malls, a perfect cold coffee (less sugary), the crust of samosa stuck on my beard, a puppy chasing to her way back home, or a gentle touch of our hands as we walked through the footpaths of busy streets; she would soak it all in, smile to herself and move on. Sometimes she would catch me staring at her, she would raise an eyebrow at me, those perfect brown eyes left me fumbling for words. I'd quietly shake my head and curse myself for not capturing the moment.

Before she moved to Mumbai, she took me to her home. Her dad talked to me about politics and women's safety in India, while her housewife mother, who looked exactly like her, made coffee and some snacks for me. Her father wasn't happy about his daughter taking a job out of state, but I could tell her mother was secretly ecstatic.

I went to see her off at the airport, my departure gift was an album of all the pictures I had taken of her. I hoped that they would remind her how beautiful she looked when she smiled at the little things in life.

# 2. Day '2'

"Nights"

There will nights when you feel stupid for feeling anything at all after someone tells you that it's just a teenager thing and you need to get over it.

There will be nights when you take a two-hour shower so you can cry without your parents raising a question of what's wrong.

There will nights when you feel stupid for feeling anything at all after someone tells you that it's just a teenager thing and you need to get over it.

There will be nights when you lay in beds for hours replaying those the way someone's touch felt on your cheeks.

There will be nights when you cry because your favorite clothes are too small and you feel like you're evolving too fast.

There will be nights when you feel like you can't do anything right and life is just worrying you out.

There will be several nights, just don't let them define you.

# 3. Day '3'

Dear Ex- bestfriend,

When some people talk about breakups, they usually refer to romantic breakups. They talk about how they didn't see the signs, or how they tried to work things out, or how they felt an emptiness after the person was gone. Funny enough, these were all the feelings I had when our friendship ended. People don't talk about one of the hardest breakups of all — friendships.

Looking back at our friendship, I remember all of the laughs we shared, the memories, the tears, the long nights, the walks, the long conversations. I remember crying to you when I felt like nothing was going my way. I remember all of the plans we talked about for the future. Most of all, I remember how easy it was to knock on your door when I didn't want to do study anymore...but now, I walk past it like a locked room that I've lost the key for.

In the aftermath of what was left of our friendship, I had hopes that we could mend on the new weak grounds...naive of me to think that, I know. Naive of me to hope that you would realize our last argument wasn't worth ending the friendship. Naive of me to think that you would respond to my texts like you use to do in seconds. Naive of me to believe that everything that happened was my fault and my fault alone.

Naive of me to prioritize our friendship before the friendships that other people were trying to grow, because I wanted to make sure that you knew that you were a priority. Naive of me to think that I couldn't last a week without talking to you. Now, I realize that everyone comes into your life for a reason. I won't sit here and say that our friendship means nothing now, just because we are no longer best friends. I won't sit here and say that you don't mean anything to me when you do. Still, what will happen in the future between you and me, I hope you're okay. I hope you're achieving those dreams and goals we once talked about. Part of me hoped that I could be there to see all of these things unfold, but part of me realizes that it's no longer my place to stand by you. I can now walk away knowing that although I didn't get the closure from you, I have found the closure within myself.

# 4. Day '4'

Dear future lover,

I sit every morning with a cup of coffee and think about you while drinking up my coffee.

I constantly find myself wondering how lucky I will get to have someone like you in my life. Someone who can make me laugh even when we fight. Someone who makes grocery shopping experience like a journey. Someone who understands me by heart. Someone who can see all the darkness within me and point out the stars.

Make goodbyes so hard that even a hug, would make my heart soft and I will be on my knees. Be a little behind time if that's what it takes. Be a little crazy or crazier, if that's what it takes. Fall in love a little passively, if that's what it takes. When you will come... Come like a hurricane and hit me like a storm and enter in every space of my skin.

But, please be a realist, I'm worried I've dreamt a lot for us already. It's not like I'm not logical, but curtains have to be blue. Be delicate, raw, and hauntingly lovely, childishly mature, and disturbingly gentle.

Till then I'll wait. I'll wait for you with my coffee in some silent cafes.

# 5. Day '5'

To a lover from this generation,?

?

There was this one line that always got me "You're gonna fall in love so many times before you find the one you'll be with forever. So, think of it this way: you're just one broken heart closer to happily ever after."?

?

And there has not been a more precise portrayal of what goes on, nowadays. Or did earlier too, but never got accepted.?

?

It's okay to look for a lover and crave all that cute stuff. But it's also okay to focus more on your career and give all your love to yourself.?

?

In a world where you've seen your parents fighting more than being in love, or making you choose one over the other, or your lover disloyalty on you, or all those extramarital affairs. I want you to believe that the love you want, exists.?

?

That person might be stalking their crush right now, digging their self-worth in the tomb, not being aware of the fact that they deserve so much love and respect and you wanna give it to 'em.?

?

So, it's okay. Things take time. In a century, where everything/ everyone is just a click away, true love might not be. It's still going to take its time and be right there in front of you when you have understood most of your lessons and are ready to explore new ones with this person. We humans want to control everything, have an answer to all the questions, to quickly solve the problem instead of learning the lessons from it. Appreciate the beauty of what goes on around you. I know it can get hard sometimes or mostly, maybe. But I know that no sadness stays. Eventually, you move on to more important things.?

?

So focus on learning new, being you, interacting with people, reading, breathing, and living.?

?

One fine day, when the time is right and you might not even be prepared to meet the love of your life, you'll meet that love. Maybe you never thought of 'dating this person but eventually, you will. You will find those flaws so beautiful and love them more than you ever thought you could. There will be a huge bucket of love for someone so much, before. Love will find you. You'll find filling up inside you and you will question if you ever had this capacity to love. Hope. Believe. Have faith.?

# 6. Day '6'

So, as you say, what difference it'd make if we got committed?

We'd talk, laugh, play as we do today, right?

"Yes, you're right. Nothing will change between us."

What is the relationship?

It's just a Tag', that's it. And if you don't want to keep that tag with you, okay. It's not a compulsion.

We're not loving each other to show the world that we're committed And even if any day, we had to give that tag, it would be Proof or Commitment for both of us. It would be like, "Yes, you love me the same as I do."

Okay, so when we should give a relationship tag? When we just want to tell the world about us. Or else I won't mind loving you without that tag.

Trust increases, your right on me and mine on you increases. The real fun of being in a relationship is truly experienced as it's different to share and fight with your friends and your siblings, the same goes for your partner. So, people want to keep that 'Tag'. And I seriously don't need that tag if you love me the same as I do.

Because the value of relationships can never change by giving it any name.

But so it is not like we should not name it or let it continue the same.

# 7. Day '7'

Happiness is not a direction, It's a place, people told me, I seem to have stuck in one awry place, and I've got lost along the way.

I am just a fighter, battling against my sanity,

and just when I think I have gained a victory, my emotions stab me from behind.

Some people love me a lot, when I talk to them or hand around with them, I feel happy for a while, but once I'm alone with my thoughts, I miss how to get happy.

I revolted my thoughts every night, But there is a threshold to how far you can bend, I'm no longer wishing for new starts, I'm just waiting for the stop.

I tried to overcome the grief, alone, on threatening late nights, I cried, I cried so badly with no one by my side, I have tried so hard to stop everything, so if I ever give up finally, just think of that I really tried my best. I tried more than my capacities. When I lose the fight against myself, swear to me that you won't sob, you'll just accept that I was tired, and murmur to my spirit adieu, okay?

# 8. Day '8'

I wanna wake up next to you, every day, I wanna feel your legs entangled with mine, every morning. I want to mildly wipe out the messed up hair falling on your sleepy face, kiss you ever so softly, and carefully untangle myself from you. I wouldn't want to wake you up. But if you mutter something in your sleep, hug my arm, and refuse to let me go, I will lie down beside you and put my arms around you. The world can wait outside our room.

I wanna stand next to you at the bus stop, listen to your jokes about work, or that unbelievable costly black outfit you've been saving up for.... and although those things may not make a point to me, may not interest me, I will listen to you ever so patiently, because I love to hear the sound of your voice when you talk about something excitedly... and if the sun glows on you too hard, I will stand in its way, I will keep you in my shadow.

I wanna stand up on the entrance for you when I hear you step on the stairs when you come house late from work. If someday I don't have an office.. and I'm struggling hard on my $4^{th}$ book, I'd love to cook you those your favorite dish and try to make just like your mother cooked for you. sit you down on the sofa and do things to you that'll make you pass over all the tension of the day. I'll let you drink your favorite wine and sip my coffee with you, listen to the stories of your childhood, the boy who broke your heart ( and secretly thank him in my heart for being dumb enough to leave you ) and carry you to bed and hug you to sleep.

...and I promise, when you wake up the next morning, you'll find me there sleeping next to you.

# 9. Day '9'

And if I stayed up with you
The whole night, talking about life,
Would you ever include my name?
And if I tell you about my dreams,
Would you like to be a part of them?
And if I'm ready to give my whole,
Would you be able to do the same?
And if I got lost in this terrible world,
Would you remember me for a while?
And if I hurt you someday unknowingly
Would you remember, how I made you smile?
And if you feel like
There's no way to come together,
Would you imagine a horizon with me?
Would you?

# 10. Day '10'

Dear You,

It's never been a piece of cake with you. Loving isn't the easiest thing. It never was it never will. Those who say that loving is the easiest thing I guess they never known love.

We fight a lot. We fight like cats and dogs, sometimes. It gets awful, up to a point where I just become so furious and say some random crap, up to the point where you keep decline my calls. It gets offensive when we shout at each other at the top of our voice. Harming each other where we know it wouldn't harm most. It gets cold like cold winds on the Kailash peaks when the storm has settled and we are sitting in a bistro facing each other trying our best to suppress the mum tears.

Sometimes, it's your blunder and mostly it's my mess.

But, I really wanna tell you that on those days when we become our worst selves and misunderstanding creates distance between us feels like two different worlds, there isn't any moment when I mourn about us. There isn't a moment when I feel like I should talk to someone else rather than you. You know why?

Because when the sun comes up the next morning I find you curled up in your corner, asleep with the tears dried up on your cheeks, the first thing I do is drift the distance between us, cover you up with a blanket. Because I know how fast you catch a cold. Because when I wake up much later in the day, I find breakfast waiting for me near my bed. Because you know my morning tea cravings. Because you know how to deal with whenever my migraine comes.

So the next time you fight with me, know this. When you call me in the middle of the night just because you can't sleep even though we cut the call a few minutes before and you don't have anything to talk about. I will be there to listen to your silence and snores...

# 11. Day '11'

love is waking up and rolling over to the right side of the bed to find someone holding you by your little finger and sleeping like a baby.

love is working hard the entire day in the office only to walk back house together, hand in hand, drinking up a cup of coffee and discussing how was the day.

love is cooking our favorite dinners together on weekends and dine it like there is no tomorrow.

love is hearing to ed sheeran on a friday night and dancing away to the tune.

love is cracking stupid jokes only to make each other laugh so hard that the nose starts watering and not just the eyes.

love is singing lame songs and sharing lame jokes.

love is clicking ugly pictures of each other and saving that as wallpaper.

love is learning comfort in each other's arms every night as we drift off to sleep.

love is treating each other like a very ordinary human being.

love is ordinary in the most extraordinary ways.

# 12. Day '12'

dear first love.

it all started with the hopelessness of getting in a relationship, bringing a girl into my world, doing the cheesiest thing we see in music and films, and turned out doing all those things besides a surprising one i.e. falling in love.

remember the late-night gossips when the conversations never ended with a 'goodbye' but with your dad coming into your room, you wrote up my all school assignments with your stunning handwriting and wrote down "mine" at the end of the page of every notebook, the few message packs where we created and shared unlimited memories, and the steps on those empty roads filled with our awkward pauses.

we had never kissed each other, yet i never skipped a single chance to hold your hands, to feel your touch although I do remember the awkward hug we had and the fastened heartbeats of yours.

i won't blame you for anything or cancer. so let's just blame fate and cherish the best times we've had with each other. i hope you're in a better place now and watching me up from there and smiling that i still think of you, sometimes.

today, whenever i go back to my hometown and walk through those roads with someone, somewhere i wish that it was you, filling all the awkward silences we've had between us.

yours sincerely,
childhood love.

# 13. Day '13'

Winters and you

i wanna go out with you in these sunny winters.

out to a snowy region, away from our homes in a small house made of woods, which will keep us warm in these autumn chills.

i wanna see the crystalline snowflakes running down your hair and want to tell you that just like how these falling snowflakes filled up the entire garden, you filled my life with happiness just by being a part of it.

i wanna play dragon wars with the vapours coming out of our mouths.

i wanna see your cheeks turning pink and the warmth in your smile, when I'll read out the poetries which I wrote for you when you'll be sleeping, laying your head on my shoulder.

i wanna pretend to be injured by the snowballs you'll throw at me, so your soft hands would touch mine and there will be another reason for the goosebumps this time.

sitting around the bonfire, singing your favourite songs for you and doing a bizarre dance on them, just to see you laugh a little louder making you forget all your pains for that moment.

i wanna sit with you beside the river tickling your palm in the same way the fishes would be tickling your feet.

i'll be your blanket when you'll be shivering out of the cold and will serve you coffee with one sugar cube, just the way you like it.

to sit with you on the roof, under the sapphire sky and billions of stars, in the warm blanket with our fingers intertwined with you resting your head on my shoulder.

i'll try my best to make the winters memorable for you because you love winters and I love you.

# 14. Day '14'

to the lover who broke my heart,

i believed it from the beginning that our relationship would last long and you always kept me doubting my beliefs, as i also believed every single word you said.

unlike other breakups, mine didn't reflect on my social media with sad captions and sympathies from the people whom barely I've talked to. i still remember that picture on my feed with a caption quoting "forever." hahaha, who knew that the continuous loop of forever would be cut down somewhere in between?

you sent me voice notes saying "i love you" to cover up for your mistakes because you were afraid of confronting and still i believed in you like a fool, every single time.

i patented for the courtesy for all the beautiful pictures of yours, which perhaps you never mentioned because i thought you didn't want people to know how close we were, which i thought was a good thought until i realised that you never wanted me to know that we can never be together.

i always had this nightmare that you'd leave me for someone better. but dreams do come true, so do nightmares. i hope you don't do this again with the person you now call your love.

with nothing but a void,

love,

the person you taught to never love.

# 15. Day '15'

it was 4 in the afternoon. i woke-up from my one-hour nap and was very much excited because it was india vs pakistan at 7 PM. i didn't wanna miss it, at any cost. i washed my face, prepared coffee, made frankie rolls, and then sat on my sofa when i gave attention to the custom notification that i had set for her whatsapp message.

the message was: "harshit, come to my place, asap!!"

i texted her back "are you okay?"

however, before i could ask her the further question she went offline and the grey tick remained single.

i went to her place, i took one silk chocolate for her because that's the only chocolate she likes the most.

she unlocked the door. she was in her favorite sweatshirt and dolphin shorts and her hair was messy flawlessly the way i admired them.

she took me to her balcony. it was almost 6:20 and the sun was about to set. i have always loved her balcony and she knew it pretty well. the setting sun, the pink sky, the tickling wind, and the two of us. it was quite alluring for me. everything was going very nicely and suddenly she held my hand. i looked into her brown eyes. they seemed like they wanted me to leave, neither her place nor her life. she hugged me so tightly and we were standing there for 5-7 minutes when she suddenly said,

"let's go make some runs because kohli can't bear the entire load on himself, mr verma."

i smiled at her and gave her a gentle kiss on the forehead when she noticed the silk i kept in my pocket. pulling it from my pocket she ran to the living room.

i turned on the tv, she got some snacks and we sat on the couch and I start concentrating on the match when she murmured in my ears, "always if you're with me,"

i didn't get it at that moment but then i understood and looked at my whatsapp and the single grey tick has turned into two blue ones.

# 16. Day '16'

to the girl who left,

i had my finger crossed when I told you that i love you. you were sitting right in front of me motionless. from those fingers crossed to entwine fingers with each other while crossing the road, we fell in love.

do you remember that morning when you woke up and rushed into my arms? and later you told me that you had a really horrible nightmare.

no, i don't think you remember any of those. but, i do. how can i pass over your smile that turned into sparkle and those gloomy eyes which made me feel you're reticent at heart? You were shivering. my touch made you even more worried before we did it. i tucked your hair behind your ears. i pulled you even closer. and then i kissed you. i could feel you shaking. the moment when I stopped my lips from yours you gripped your arms around mine. that moment i felt like falling into the world of love we made.

i saw you eating your favorite chicken biryani. it reminded me of that midnight when you had this craving for biryani and we went to every closed shop and finally got one. even your cramps couldn't stop you from what you wanted. but today, when i saw that guy standing beside you sharing your favorite chicken biryani my heartache. it felt like someone stabbed me with arrows.

i felt my stomach falling when i saw you eating from his plate. i wondered how many more times you would be saying "i love you" to him. about where i lacked; those hugs, kisses, or maybe the love. your reasons were preposterous. your ruse heart only wanted to get rid of my devoted love.

our vows we rendered among which hanging around beside each other no matter what was the gigantic agony i dream of every day. your hair clips, that red nail paint, that letter, that hoodie, that diary, and your half-finished ice cream. so just come for the last time and take it, take it all even our memories.

from,

someone who loved you truly.

# 17. Day '17'

it was the first time I was going to her house to spend an entire night. i left my hostel and purchased burgers, some packets of chips, and vanilla ice-cream as it was the runner-up in the list of her favorite things.

it was a pretty cold night cause it's the month of december, i reached her place at 8:00 PM. as i was about to ring the bell she just opened the door like she was waiting for me badly, and my eyes stuck on her, I actually kept on staring at her for the past 15-20 seconds. she was looking extremely beautiful in her white colour oversized tee with her favorite grey shorts. ?she had left her hair open and was standing at some distance from me, yet I could smell the fragrance of her perfume. her eyes, ah, her eyes never failed to mesmerize me, and her chubby cheeks have this light pink because of the weather which makes her astonishing.

?

no, she was not 'snow-white' but she was looking perfect in every different way.? she went to the kitchen to finish what she was preparing for me it was our favorite alfredo pasta and in the meantime, I went to her gallery. ?

?

after two minutes two hands gently wrapped my waist from behind and my body could feel the beating of another heart on it. i could smell the same fragrance but barely at a distance of few a inches. ?we were standing on her balcony and gazing at the moon together.?

?

then suddenly she asked.?
"i don't know which moon is more beautiful the one which is up in the sky, or the one who is sitting with me.?"
"the moon in the sky is always beautiful no matter what but you will have this one on every new moon and in every situation, you will be through." i continued.?

?

"she blushed,"
we were standing under a night full of stars and our souls were totally into each other.?
"don't worry you're the only sun I take my glow from,"
i smirked and looked at her.?
little did I know, that I turned the light pink into a totally red one.

?

# 18. Day '18'

he is the one who makes you feel better when you are reluctant without you having to ask for anything.?

?

he goes out of his way just to make you laugh to get a glimpse of your happiness because it makes him happy.?

?

he is fun to be around without having to go somewhere fancy because you just enjoy being around him and you enjoy his company in itself.?

?

he gives you a sweatshirt that smells like him without you having to ask him for it and tells you that you look better than him in it.?

?

he recalls you every day that you are precious even when you feel like shit and tells you that he loves you for who you are.?

?

he makes you feel comfortable and protected and gives you the warmest hugs.

?

he opens up to you about his crises, emotions, listens, and cares about what you have to say even if it's just about how your day went and he will do anything he can to make it

better and he is capable of doing so simply by smiling at you.?
he may not be perfect for other people but perfect in your eyes
and that's all that matters.?

# 19. Day '19'

letter from a prostitute to society,

i started this at the age of 30 when my husband died due to excessive drinking. i was an unemployed, vulnerable widow. we weren't in contact with any of our families as everyone was against our love marriage. who'd marry a woman who's been raped and yet accused as culpable?

i started exploring jobs to do for my survival, i applied for babysitting, housemaid, but the stain on my character didn't get me anywhere.

i was going on out of money when I went to this person's house to apply for the job of a housemaid. he opened the door and before I could utter a word out of my mouth, i saw him staring at me, his eyes moving all over my body. my body shook out of fear for a second. those eyes, that gaze, had been through me before and now I knew what was getting to.

i went inside his house, he started asking me questions and in the middle of the talk, he started touching me indecently. i tried to stop him a few times but then he offered me money. i got stuck in a catastrophe because money was everything needed then for my survival, but I had never thought that I'd have to sell my body for that. he started touching me once again but this time I didn't stop him.

he handed over to me the agreed amount of money and I went home, crying. but at least now I was able to buy some food and my essentials. two weeks later, I started getting calls from many unknown men asking for prostitution. and before moving toward the police I gave this thing, a second thought.
1) what if nothing else worked for me?
2) what if this prostitution thing helped to satisfy the thirst of these sexual predators and would result in a decrease in the number of rape crimes?
3) what if I could save someone's life?
i don't wish to undo the decision I took that day, i may not be obeyed in society, but I'm happy that I'm surviving, I'm happy that I didn't give up on myself.
"nevertheless, we don't do it out of choice, we do it because we don't have a choice."
yours unwelcomed,
the woman who craves some respect.

# 20. Day '20'

"okay, tell me what do you wanna be, in your next life?" i
asked her

"i want to have the power to fly," she replied.

"fly?? like an airplane? all that they do is fly." i said stupidly.

"no, you idiot. not like an airplane. like a bird." she laughs.

"alright. why?" i questioned.

"i know it sounds cliche, but it is beautiful. there is freedom in
it. you carry around all the problems and pieces of baggage in
the world and then keep on wondering what's making you feel
thick. you are always on the ground just trying to put things
behind you and feel that flow of air in your wings when you
fly high. maybe I have seen too many films, you know...
with a smile still, on her face, she begins again,
but this is what I want to be. a bird flying over an ocean with
her flock, in the backdrop of an orange sun and a pink sky.
moments where you could just forget all your grief and float
in the way the wind blows and be happy with where you are
at."

"damn! that was pretty deep," i mumbled while gazing into
her eyes.

"i know. so what about you, harshit?" she asked.

"a god," i answered back while thinking something.

"what? you can't be god, harshit. c'mon answer me seriously."

"but, that's what I wanna be in my next life. what's the problem?" i asked her.

"you can't be. only humans are reborn and not gods. they're constant. think of something else now. c'mon harshit, you're a writer tell me something good naa," she said with her potato face.

"that's not really fair," i told her.

"i don't know, just think," she said.

"okay."

"so...?" she looked at me.

"i think I'd want to be a god," i repeated.

"again..? why? why are you glued on it? what do you wanna do being a god?" she said with anger.

"to make you a bird,"

# 21. Day '21'

i remember looking into her eyes, and god this feeling won't tune down a bit.

"tiny peck on her cheeks would do," i think to myself.

"okay... ready!" she is looking at me.

her eyes! oh, god. those beautiful crescent eyes. it's sparkling with joy and the happiness in them alone tells me what she needs right now.

i tell her something stupid and god bless her, for she finds every silly thing I say, funny and then she laid to rest her face on my chest, smiling. her hairs slipping down from behind her ear and falling over her face. damn!!! she's the most beautiful thing I have ever set my eyes on.

i trace the line of her face, gazing over her jaw, her cheeks. she's elegant. she has always been this elegant. her head over my chest aroused a dark desire inside me, unlike anything I have experienced before.

i take my face near hers. i don't imagine how the way she smells can affect me so deeply, but yes it does. like I remember her from another birth.

her hands clasped on my chest. i can sense her breathes reaching down my body through my t-shirt. i didn't wait another minute.

falling down my lips on her cheeks, I kissed her. the warmest and the sweetest thing, I have ever tasted.

she looks up at me.

her eyes singing to me, the pulse of my heart beneath her hand right now. she leans in and kisses me in return.

the world overclouded into white. there was only me, she, this kiss, and nothing more. i take in more of her smell like I wanna be submerged with her aroma.

i cannot feel my legs. they left boneless.

i wanted to hold her close like she was my gigantic support pillar that was gonna vanish any time. she smelled like earth and rain. my heart began to run out of my body creeping into every nerve of me. i look at her, cup her face with my hands, stare into her stunning eyes for a few seconds. we smile at each other.

i can feel the vibes flickering out of her, I can feel them meeting mine, the friction, the aggressiveness, the passion, the desire, and the love embraced each other as we had our smiles colliding. i can probably not write this down.

i can probably never stop recalling these moments. the moments where I held my dreams in my captivity and kissed it.

# 22. Day '22'

having a sister is something that can have its moments of absolute chaos, but is ultimately one of the greatest gifts the world has to offer. and when you have a sister as inspiring as mine that teaches you so many valuable life lessons, it is even more precious.?

?

who you really are, is good enough...?

?

a lot of things that we do in life are for other people whether it be the way we act or the places we go to. one of the coolest things about siblings is that you do not ever have to be anything or anyone but exactly who you are. they never expect you to be "on" all the time because they aren't either. you never have to try to impress them, because they have already seen you at your worst. it's a reassuring feeling to know that there is a person in this world who truly knows you inside and out and still loves you. they taught me that whoever the world tries to make me, I can still be me.?

?

time doesn't have to change anything...?

?

whenever I go home, I kind of expect to be treated like royalty (which never happens). while my sisters always greet me with excitement, after a few minutes together we are already arguing over where to eat or what to watch on tv. i am thankful for this normality. it takes a special kind of person to be able to pick up right where you left off, and sisters can do that, no matter what has happened or how long it's been. they taught me that time doesn't change situations, we do.?

?

hearing the truth is refreshing...?

?

someone who tells you exactly how it is is not something you find every day. most of the time, what we want to hear and what we need to hear are not the same things. sisters really have nothing to lose. If you get mad at them you can't just stop talking to them...because they are family. hearing the brutally honest truth can be tough, but sometimes we need that. they taught me that no matter how hard it is to hear, someone will always be there to say it.?

?

sometimes you have to let go...?

?

i think anyone who has siblings would agree that you'd do just about anything for them. i feel protective of them because they are such a huge part of who I am.

growing up I know I made mistakes, mistakes I wish I wouldn't have and I don't want to let them do the same...but sometimes they have to. it's hard for me, as my sisters grow up, to watch them make some of the same mistakes I did, and I want to do everything in my power to stop them from making them. i have learned that sometimes, them learning a lesson from their screw-ups is more valuable than me interfering. they taught me that sometimes sitting back and saying nothing is the most effective way to learn.?

?

it might be a bad day, but it's not a bad life...?

?

no matter what I face throughout the day, a bad result, a toxic ex, or if I just feel like the world is against me, I have one people that are the best reminder of all that is good in this life. the family has a way of helping those bad days not seem so bad and putting it all in perspective. the life lessons that I continue to learn from them will help me as I navigate this journey called life and I am thankful to have my elder sister along for the ride.?

# 23. Day '23'

she loves how he holds her.

she loves how he tells her that she's beautiful.

she loves how he makes her happy.

she loves how he smiles when she sees him from a distance.

she loves how he asks her if she's alright when she can't stop laughing.

she loves how he makes her feel.

she loves how he likes her in shorts, messy hair, and in his favorite shirt.

she loves how he says sweet things to her.

she loves how he whispers so quietly at the restaurant table that the over-inquisitive aunty beside couldn't hear a thing.

she loves how she can talk to him for hours about anything, and he listens and just listens to her without any complaint.

she loves how they call each other as soon as they wake up.

she loves how he wants to spend most of his time with her.

she loves how he rubs her back while hugging and kisses her neck.

she loves how he lays next to her, and tell her that everything is so perfect.

she loves how he sees the person she really is with all her imperfection.

she loves how he says they are perfect for each other.

she loves how he makes her cry, but not because she feels sad, or he hurt her, but because he made her the happiest person ever.

she loves how he kisses her and gives a soft bite on her cheeks.

she loves how he thinks she has cute feet.

she loves how she looks at the empty space in her bed and wishes he was feeling it.

she loves how she gets nervous when she sees him but feels more comfortable with him than she does with anyone else.

she loves how he concerns about her and takes care of her.

she loves how he tries to pay for her when they go places.

she loves how he claims everything will be alright and make her feel at ease.

she loves how he keeps her warm when she's cold.

she loves how he gives her bizarre looks at awkward moments.

she loves how he stops everything for her. she loves how she's important to him.

she loves how she makes him happy.

she loves how he gets jealous when she tells him that she saw her ex and talked a little bit.

she loves how they talk about being together forever.?

she loves how she can see her with him forever.

??

she loves everything about him.??

# 24. Day '24'

i don't think I know what love is.
is it the way my eyes light up when I see you?
with that smile that brightens a room,
is it the way my heart speeds up when we touch?
with a touch that awakens my soul,
is it the twinkle in your eyes?
when the sun hits them just right,
or is it that subtle smile that crosses my face whenever we talk?
i don't think I know what love is.
maybe it's the way my fingers fit perfectly between yours.
maybe it's the electricity that shocks me when we kiss.
maybe it's your laughter echoing through my heart,
or the way you let me talk for hours and let me sleep on a
video call.
i don't think I know what love is.
is it the way you talk to me?
with a language of our own,
is it the way you chose me over others?
all the other girls are prettier than me.
is it the way we share secrets?
Our deepest thoughts,
or is it the comfort of your arms?
i don't think I know what love is.

maybe it's the shivers that appear at your touch.

maybe it's the way you look at me from across the room.

maybe it's the way you tickle me nonstop,

or is it the way I think of you for hours?

i think I know what love is.

it's the way you hold me,

your arms feel like home.

it's the way you kiss my forehead,

ever so lightly.

it's the way we can just sit without words,

quiet but loud with the beating of our hearts.

it's the way I still get nervous to see you,

my heart's unending excitement.

love is the butterflies in the pit of my stomach.

love is the way we just watch the stars,

love is the way the world fades away when I am with you,

love is the way God has graced me with you.

love is the endless heartache I'll feel,

love is the undying emotions,

love is not judging.

love is dedication,

love is seeing an imperfect person as perfect,

yaa... I think that is love.

# 25. Day '25'

do you remember the rooftop?

i do.

i remember all the sundowns, how we would sit and watch the world from over.

how the golden dome in front of us would be submerged in the colors of the sun during the sunsets. how as we talked, we'd watch the flock of birds fly one back to their homes or maybe fly in search of a new one.

we would always argue on that.

although I still believe they're going back home.

i hope they are.

of all the moments, I remember the last evening we spent on the roof the most.

you were in your black dress and you kept saying that it made you look fat.

it didn't. it fits you perfectly as if it was made for you. there were little white flowers printed on it and you were pretty sure that they smelled like a bunch of jasmines.

i remember your giggle when I tried to smell one. i think I can still hear it, right now while I'm on this rooftop with my new girlfriend.

yeah. ten years after your death, I've finally decided to move on.

I've known her quite long now and we'll soon be committed I guess. but for some reason, I wanted to bring her here before we do.

and guess what?

she loves the view too.

although I don't.

from up here, the world ain't that beautiful anymore.

i don't see birds.

the sun has almost set, but the dome doesn't shine like it used to.

When the sun is gone, the sky is now pink, with little white clouds floating around.

and you know, maybe you were right.

i do smell jasmines now.

# 26. Day '26'

i hope you find someone who would get you chocolates and still manage to call you sweet by some cheesy lines.

the one who'll forget his keys just to have another glance at you, to look into your eyes, to see your smile.

the one who'll send you the worst pictures of himself without having a fear of being judged and will listen to your voice clips, over and again.

the one who'll wrap you snugly in his sweatshirt, tickle you often just to have another tight grip of yours.

who will fall for your heart, the way you smile, the way you treat people, the way you fall asleep on his shoulders and your eyes would be his favorite color.

whose voice would haunt you at 3 AM and think of losing him will leave your dawns sleepless.

the one who'd be grateful for your presence in his life and will love your imperfections.

i hope you get the love, you think you deserve because now I won't be that person, not anymore.

# 27. Day '27'

it was our 75<sup>th</sup> anniversary and I wanted to make it special for her this time.

i wanted to thank her for everything she has done for me and everything she has been for me; a caring mother, a beautiful wife, and a perfect soulmate.

i went to the florist to buy some flowers for her. she loved the red roses and it looked perfect on her untied long hair making them look more gorgeous.

later on, I went to the place where we usually meet. She was waiting for me with the same Yardley bottle of her favorite perfume I gifted her on our last anniversary.

i went closer, and before she could utter a single word out of disheartenment, I went on knees and said,

thank you for always looking for me whenever I lost myself and searching for me.

thank you for always become the only ear who can listen to me when I don't have anyone.

thank you for making my smile a little broader when I was completely drowned in the ocean of sorrows.

thank you for everything. I love you and I always will.

she was so quiet. I was able to listen to the wind blowing around, I could smell the fragrance of the rose, I could feel the dry leaves tickling my legs.

she was still quiet, she didn't speak a word. tears tried to peek out from my eyes but I somehow controlled them and kept a smile on my face.

i stood up handed over the rose to her and started walking away from that place.

neither did she utter a single word nor the red rose looked beautiful on her grave.

# 28. Day '28'

"it rained today, do you know that?

"yeah, I know it did," i sai

"whenever the world celebrates a new year, for the past two years, we've been here at this beach, watching the waves crash for hours. i never forced you to stay, but you did anyway

i look at her. her eyes stuck at the blue waves, while the wind plays with her hair, tossing them all over her face. while the setting sun places its orange shade on her nostalgic eyes, she nods and replie

"yeah. i've loved being here

"don't you want to talk about that night, avyah

"let's not go to that," she told m

"okay. but I can't stop thinking why would you wanna be someplace for so long when nothing has been vowe

we've never said those words to each other but then why?" i asked her

"every day before I go to sleep, I think about you, rishi. i think about us. it feels vague but good nevertheless. i hope, I pray for us. i add my one hope to another like beads on a string, to make a necklace of eternity and wear it around my neck. i hold it close before I sleep and think of you while I doze off. so I never said to you I love you because what I have for you is something much bigger and much more dangerous," she sai i feel a strong wind that poured out against me from the sea.

little waves reached her toes, tickled her feet, and lef

she giggled at the

i pull her close towards me, while she leans her back on my chest, her hands rested over my thighs. we both continue looking at the sea and watch the waves carry the sand and leave it lying beside u

placing my lips closer to her ears, i sai

"every time we were to part our ways, I always whispered to myself 'just five more seconds or maybe just sixty more'. i never said it to you, but always to myself

if I added up all the 'one mores' we'd have a boundless loop of time for ourselves. and in that loop, I'd want to hold your hand and walk to the line, where the sea meets the sun. and where this zillion of barriers end, we'll skateboard through the loop

she smiled and turns back and hugged m

I love you, rish

I love you, avyah. i.e..".d,s.m.t.d..d?e.?"."s,."d."_e likes

I love you, rishi.

I love you, avyah.

# 29. Day '29'

i really love how beautiful you make the world around you.

i really love how deeply you look into my eyes and make me realise that I matter.

i really love how you hold my hands as if to never let you go.

i really love how tightly cuddle me just like there's is no tomorrow.

i really love how catching a glimpse of you happy, fills my heart.

i really love how you always understand me, especially when I am the one at guilt.

i really love how don't you really love me, yet always love me enough.

i really love how you just let us be.

i really love what you're still to become.

i really love how you just love me.

# 30. Day '30'

we were riding the bike for more than an hour. we didn't ride far but went around the same road many times. speeding against places we already knew, at 5:30 in the evening of January. i still am not clear about how it happened.

i was in this leather jacket and she was in her pajamas. we were cracking up and screaming, shivering when the cold winds rode straight into our nerves as we moved against them.

it felt right out of a film.

we jumped a speed breaker and she held me tight

jay, that felt like turbulence."

i look back and shout at the top of my voice so that she could hear me against the gushing wind.

"what??"

"turbulence, jay. turbulence," she shouts back.

"why so?"

"because it's scary,"

i slow down.

i hear her catching her breath while she tries to suppress her smile.

i talk back.

"i don't want you to feel this like turbulence."

"then?"

"i want you to experience this like a roller-coaster."

she giggles.

"why is that?" she asks while slowly leaning her head against my shoulder.

i could feel her hands around my waist.

"because it's risky and short-lived too, just like turbulence. but, you know that it's going to be fun, you know that you're cautious and that when you are gonna get down from this, you're gonna have a broad fucking grin on your face. and that to me is beautiful."

she hugs me a little too tight while she raises her mouth to my ear to whisper back,

"i hope this roller-coaster never stops."

while accelerating up again, I reply,

"i hope the same."

# 31. Day '31'

she had a gentle, soft voice, and she told me her story.

she told me a little about her past and her future. she talks as if it were to happen tomorrow, and she does it with such sheer and absolute anticipation that it's almost potent. she's intoxicating. Intoxicating what a word to describe a human being. but she's not the two a.m. cigarette kind of intoxication. no, no. she's more like a crude mixture of lakeshore air and barn paint. nah, that does not sound good. how about the unveiling of a thousand stars as you leave the tree line of a dense forest? pure and refined intoxication. eh, not quite. i could say she has deep, dark eyes that draw you in, but that doesn't nearly describe it. imagine, a beach. the air blowing across your face. the feeling of wet sand and water mixed between your toes, and ever so often the waves washing all of it away. now look to the left of your feet. do you see the wet, dark sand with the sophisticated swirling pattern interlaced through it? that's the color of her eyes. now look to the right. the tiny feet that have pitter-pattered across the whole beach, yeah, the few foot section in front of you is just a portion of her life story she's told me, with each pair of feet representing something different she wants to do with her life. i wish I could see where they all go. now imagine it happening all at once and you may never get the chance to experience it again. that kind of intoxication.

but maybe I'm just exaggerating.

that's the problem with being a writer. we write and we write to find vague things and thoughts and twist and turn them into things we think are beautiful. then we do that same thing over and over expecting different results. then, people who think we're crying wolf don't believe us when we pick up something we think is special and say, "look! look what I've got right here! it's beautiful and special and amazing!" as we proceed to shove the said thing in their faces to prove a point. then, look at the way her eyes light up when she smiles, kind of the point. you know, the smile she makes when she brought up the coffee shop and keeping beds for the homeless.

# 32. Day '32'

maybe it's those little things that matter.

your smile, your understanding, your worst day, your best days, your saddest day, your fears, your tears, your dimple, your pimple, your happiness, your craziness, your care, your love, and your friendship.

every little thing that brings a smile on your face a bit is everything that matters.

your presence, your innocent face when you make, your messy hair that looks beautiful in its peculiar way, your gentle face when you see your favorite food in front of you, your tired smile on your drooping face before the sun sets, your sleepy voice and your morning face.

a shoulder to cry on and those beautiful eyes to sparkle up your darkest times.

yes, that's all that really matters.

not everyone can define you but your people and you know who you are and that's what really matters.

# 33. Day '33'

if I was a teacher, I would say you were the easiest math question to solve, after searching for the answer online.

if I was a magician, I would say you were my favorite trick to perform because I was told how to do it in the matric.

if I was a bird, I would say you were the tallest tree I ever perched on because I've only ever landed on you.

if I was a bee, I would say you were the best smelling rose I ever landed on, even though you're my first rose of the day.

if you were a drug, I would say I was a recovering drug addict, and then I'd snort you.

if you were wet leaves, I would say I was a tree, and grow you again.

if you were a moth, I would say all lights off and keep candlelit.

if we were honest, I would say that I barely know you.

if we were in love I would say, for how long?

if we were in a movie, I would say there is no sequel.

if I keep thinking about us, I would say that I may care.

if I was four years younger, I would say this was easy.

it's difficult to know what I would say if someone asked, what's going on?

i would probably say, that you were the moon and I was the sun and that we wait patiently for the eclipse.

# 34. Day '34'

firsts are always valuable.

first words, first school, the first day of college, first trip, first touch, first love, first kiss, first heartbreak, first job, first salary, first this or first that, first everything.

so when all my friends celebrated their firsts with someone, I was always present to celebrate with them. it hurt standing alone but there was always hope.

so it won't be a shocker when I say my most memorable moment was when someone showed interest in me. for the first time.

i remember her brown eyes, her beautiful smile, her pink cheeks and the way she talks is something that I talk about a lot. i can never forget the night we talked for god knows how long and I will also never forget the two little blue ticks on my "hey!"

# 35. Day '35'

there is this girl I know, who smiles distinctly whenever she tells stories of her first childhood love. that innocent, sweet, and pure type.

there is this girl I know who treats street dogs like her own babies.

she talks about those iconic games, shows, places, things, and most importantly people, she cherishes. you can sense the excitement in her voice when she talks about all those things that really matter to her and you find a little grief in her voice too when she talks about the person she never thought will leave her life and become some strangers.

there is this girl I know, who thinks she is so mature but her voice makes you feel like she is just a school kid.

there is this girl I know, who is more of an introverted person who would never tell you anything if you don't initiate or ask her any things. but you do ask her she will tell you everything and let you know that her dadu was the closest one and how she secretly misses him sometimes and sob while standing on the balcony.

there is this girl I know, who will ask you to smile and let go of all the worries and grudges and forgive everyone even the person who is your enemy.

the one who will tell you to be kind not just to others but to yourself too. she will talk about life and tell you why you must make it worth living.

there is this girl I know, who is a little bit stubborn when it comes to things she doesn't wanna share.

there is this girl I know, if you'll look at her you will realise that innocence can have a face too and when you will know things what she had done for the people you start believing that humanity still exists.

there is this girl I know, who is now in love with herself more than anyone else.

# 36. Day '36'

she was like a magical gift that destiny has gifted me. I will be there in her hard times and definitely will help to get her out of it or we both face it together.

she doesn't know how much I love her. I have never shown up to her to the fullest because whatever I did for her, she was so satisfied with that.

maybe...

maybe I love her too hard.

maybe I love her too selflessly.

maybe she doesn't have any idea about how much I love her.

maybe I expect too much from her.

maybe I deserve too less.

maybe I am the star and she was searching for the moon.

maybe she loves me but doesn't wanna show me.

and that's the only thing I will ever wanna know.

i will try to busy myself with some stuff that I do but whenever I take a pause, I think of her.

every little thing that we shared, every glance, is still saved in the back of my mind.

no matter how much she tried to make me forget them, their existence is inescapable.

more than losing her, the thought of living alone terrifies me.

she is a combination of crazy, calm, intelligent, elegant and i love her.

# 37. Day '37'

if there's one thing I've realised, it's that everyone is damaged.
unbelievably torn apart. ripped to shreds even.
what's the point in trying to heal everyone. most people will
reject the fact that there is something that haunts the back of
their minds.
because maybe if they don't say it, it won't be true. but the
truth is, everyone has their demons.
the only thing we can do is offer the good parts of us and hope
they dance well with the bad parts.
if you're going to love someone, you have to fall in love with
their moon and their sun.
it's your responsibility to love them even when the only thing
shining in their eyes is a relentless moon.
love them until the sun comes out.

# 38. Day '38'

leaving has been always been something I'm really good at. ??

??leaving places, leaving people, leaving homes, leaving cities, leaving love. ??

??i never believed in roots. ??

??roots kept me stuck in one place. ??

??i hated being stuck. ??

i've always been this way. no, excuse no, apologies. ??

i've been letting go for as long as I can remember. ??

because frankly, I don't remember anything before I met you.??

??i don't remember anything before I lost you. ??

before you left... and when you left, I was stuck in one place for a very long?? long time, a place I don't want to recollect, re-visit. ??

??ever since I got out and its miracle I did, all I have ever done is run, away from you, away from everything that makes me want me to build a home.??

??see I had a home. i watched it burn down all around me.??

??i pulled myself out of the burning debris. ??

??not you. ??

??you weren't there. ??

??you left me, too busy saving yourself. ??

??that's when I learned to do my own savings. ??

??that's when I learned to be alone.??

• 65 •

# 39. Day '39'

there is a unique way you smile when you tell me stories of your adolescence. on those tiring out weekends, sitting at our favorite bistro.

you talk about things you love through lips bitter from black coffee, and I watch your eyes light up like a city on a diwali night. you tell me of the time your dad took your family on this trip to the maldives. it was your first vacation with your family. you were eight.

you tell me of men who you've loved. men who loved you while you didn't love them back. you tell me about this one guy who meant the world to you. how he used to sing songs for you that would take your breath away. how he was so very difficult to be with, so very different from everyone else you've ever met. you never wanted easy, did you?

you tell me how you haven't spoken to him in years, how you're not in love with him anymore. i notice how you stare at the things and lost somewhere yourself, while you talk about him.

what do you see? do you wonder where he is now, what is he doing, is he okay? is he happy?

there is a certain way your eyes light up when you talk about the things you love. like the sun setting on a faraway city, its last rays lighting up a tiny cafe at the edge of a highway,

where a man sits at a window-side table... doodling on a tissue
paper. he puts his pen down and looks up, to where the sky
has turned lilac-blue. his tired eyes search for something across
the horizon. he remembers.. and smiles to himself.
the waitress walks up to him...
"your order sir!"
he rouses from his dream.
"cappuccino, with extra cream and a blueberry cheesecake,"
the smile still lingers on his lips.

# 40. Day '40'

we've been here so several times for me to think back to now. i guess we have sat almost on every slate of this rooftop. i awe how many people have sat on the same slates as we have and share stories as we did. how many cried. how many smiled. I'll always wonder.

college is done. and now you're gone.

well, we always knew we didn't have a forever. we were just two broken souls who just expected a love story for themselves. we just wished to live a fairytale, make some memories and leave. remember we wrote down our bucket list?

i still have it. right now in my wallet. i know it by heart. we didn't do all of it and there are still five remaining . "embrace our best memories and let them bring sorrow to you," you always used to say. i can feel it now. i know we fought so much for the kind of life, we didn't have time to live.

our last night together?

i never slept. i was awake the entire time looking at you. watching the sunrise on you. because I knew this is probably the last time I'd ever see this. that the next day, this would be a memory.

we both knew this was gonna be dangerous. when it all started, but we did it either way. just like two flies jovially flying towards the fire.

but I thank you. i thank you for all the smiles, the days, the nights. for teaching me that we can love and still let go. for teaching me that, we can have an endless love story duration of just few years.

# 41. Day '41'

there are various kinds of loneliness. and I think I've been through each of them.

this is probably just a new one. wherein, it isn't about being lonely, but just empty. my thoughts are empty, my reality, my reasons, everything. the depth of nothingness lingers around so hard, that it's almost impossible not to spot it. i don't know. maybe it is because I miss you, or maybe it's because I keep thinking about, how along with you, what I lost isn't something that I can put under one umbrella, but so many small things spread over a big spectrum and this loneliness is just a big space of where they all used to once fit.

maybe it is because our goodbyes weren't perfect. they weren't tucked beneath the blues of sorrow or weren't tainted with the reds of fury. but just walked up to us, slow-paced yet powerful, like a bad dream. if we had anticipated it, we would have known. we would have awaited the blow of it. but no. our goodbyes came calmly yet unexpectedly, intertwined with bad times and situations.

maybe because it was unexpected, there's still a strong, needling pain. the pain where we couldn't mourn what we lost and what died between us, within us.

the pain always makes me long and makes me wonder about what could have been. and I think ours would have been a beautiful story, but all that it now is incomplete poetry. and I guess that's what the emptiness is about. the words we forgot to write together in our book.

• 71 •

# 42. Day '42'

sometimes your friends get sad and you can't help them. be it because a friend of theirs has left and you just aren't the voice they want to hear. perhaps they are drunk and determined to find that certain someone who calls them pretty, or they just have some problems in their personal life. no matter what, sometimes your words just don't help even if they have previously. people get lost in their heads a lot and it can take a lot to pull them back out, but even sitting with someone in silence can be what they need. there have been many moments where I sat in silence on one end of the phone listening to a friend cry because that's all I could do for him or her.

sometimes you get sad for no reason and you need to just ride it out for a few minutes. today I was listening to music and eating dinner and suddenly, i felt like I needed to cry. it wasn't that anything was wrong or that anything had happened, it was just a moment where things suddenly weren't good for a few minutes. these moments are random, but there isn't really anything to do besides riding it out. you can go get your favorite food, sit with a friend, but these things aren't going to make it go away. sometimes you just have to be sad.

shit happens, really bad shit that shakes you to your core. life has a way of coming at you with situations you desperately hoped would never occur and you can't stop it. you adapt and pick up the pieces and cry a lot and keep going because that's how life is. no one is lucky enough to get through life without obstacles and some of us get a bunch of them thrown at us all at once, but take a deep breath and keep going.

life has a not-so-great way of reminding us that a lot of things are possible and the best we can do is make sure we can keep going. it's not possible to be prepared or to fix every situation, so take a deep breath and remember that it's okay to cry. now I am okay and eating a box of white sauce pasta, but I know that I'm preparing well for my exams and that my family and friends are doing okay, so I'll be okay too.

# 43. Day '43'

let's just imagine,
what would you say if I told
you let's be friends
that take long late night walks
and dance in the middle of the empty streets,
grasping cold air on warmed skin,
arms out, flying and falling over words
let's just imagine,
what would you say if I asked
you on a date
nights on the couch, head on your lap
wearing your favorite shirt, untangling my curly hair
with skeptical fingers
whispering "you should tell me to stop"
let's just imagine,
what would you say if I asked
you for a kiss
because your lips look like they would fit against mine
two pieces of a riddle fitting together with that little click
a gunshot of adrenaline going off with that little click
teach my naive lips the dance every person
dreams of learning
let's just imagine,

what would you say if I asked

you for things to be serious

five pictures of us laughing, lit up by city lights

my poetry read on those nights when we're not sure

where this is going

falling along, hand entangled, lovers clasped

falling over words the other will grab

let's just imagine,

what would you say if I confessed

you to loving you

that you made my heart beats faster from day one

your giggle had me drunk

and every night, I dreamed of

kissing that silly smile off your face

i stopped believing in the myths

but I'm under your spell

this is the twisted love story I always wanted

let's just imagine,

dance on broken city streets

lips meeting in the gloomy staircase

hands tangled in pockets in the dark

stay up too late and wake up too early

get lost in each other's eyes

let sobriety act on these love drunk bones

until we can't escape each other

if your answer is one

you're not sure I want to hear,

it's okay, because
this was all imagination,
right?

# 44. Day '44'

hey there,

it's okay, it's okay if it's affecting you cause one day it will stop affecting you. i know it is really hard but it's meant to be hard you know. if it's not hard then it wasn't real. real is always painful and powerful so, deal with it.

it's okay if it affecting you more than it does to others.

it's okay if you feel more bottomless than others.

getting affecting just because the situation is very natural.

but we tend to loosen up our emotions a little bit more than usual cause these situations aren't expected.

but that's all what life is all about right?

it's mercurial.

and that's how we learn about things and we grow.

and that's how we move on.

so, if it's affecting you then let it.

that's when we learn about the things the most.

let it make you cry.

let it hurt you.

let it bleed.

let it heal.

take care of yourself.

# 45. Day '45'

it was an ordinary sunday evening. we went for a walk to the lakeside because I wanted to see the epitome of beauty. it was around six and we were eagerly waiting for the sunset. she was in a floral white dress which I gave her on her birthday because I loved the white color changing to a reddish-orange as the sun starts going down and down to meet the blue somewhere in the end.

but that day, the sky was in a mockery mood and striving to make fun of us. it was neither red nor yellow and not of the single color from 'VIBGYOR.' our full sight was surrounded by dark grey clouds, the cool wind teasing her tresses and I could spend my whole life watching her somehow manage to put them behind her ears and calling out my name for no reason.

after a few moments, it started raining. before the water droplets could ruin her straight hair which she took a few hours to set properly, we ran after looking for the shack. we were almost wet until we entered the shed and because we were wet, we stood at a distance of five feet from each other. no one of us was carrying an umbrella but for the first time, I was not regretting it.

suddenly, a bright light flashed in the gray sky with a shaky loud sound and the distance of those five feet almost vanished.

# 46. Day '46'

there was something about the way she smiled, that made the world seem a little brighter. it didn't take much to make her happy. a gentle breeze out of nowhere, a little kid selling soft toys at traffic lights, a group of sparrows feeding on crumbs at the terrace, a pup following her on her way back to home, just some random babies on malls, the crust of samosa stuck on my beard or a gentle touch of our hands as we walked through the footpaths of busy streets; she would soak it all in, smile to herself and move on. sometimes she would catch me staring at her, she would raise an eyebrow at me, those perfect brown eyes left me fumbling for words. i'd quietly shake my head and curse myself for not capturing the moment.

before she moved to mumbai, she took me to her home. her dad talked to me about politics and women's safety in India, while her housewife mother, who looked exactly like her, made coffee and some snacks for me. her father wasn't happy about his daughter taking a job out of state, but I could tell her mother was secretly ecstatic.

i went to see her off at the airport, my departure gift was an album of all the pictures I had taken of her. i hoped that they would remind her how beautiful she looked when she smiled at the little things in life.

# 47. Day '47'

hey,

these three hours after midnight are the hours when all my vulnerabilities siege me and this is when I take my mask off just to let the cries behind my smile come out. but somehow you figured out that the full stops and the exclamations meant something more than just full stops and exclamations.

it feels so good to have someone who comes upon in your vulnerabilities and pulls your soul up, rather than judging your weak points and eventually ending up becoming one of them.

i sacrifice my sleep talking to you and you pause the suspense of Ross' wedding and don't even complain about it. and this is the time when the true talk takes place.

we are a new person every day, we know each other differently, we find answers to each other's questions and sometimes we don't, because maybe we are it.

it's not the subject that keeps the conversation going on, it's the heart that oaths to stay honest and real. and who knew, the gap between 'goodnight' and 'bye' would be of two more hours.

thank you for sharing my midnight cup of coffee and being one of the sugar cubes which did not dissolve, when I actually needed it the most.

lots of love,
your 2 AM friend.

# 48. Day '48'

love her, love her hard. ?
get close to her and entwine your fingers with hers. ?
laugh at her lamest jokes.?
laugh with her. ?
remember her laughter. ?
go back to it when she is not around and you're missing her.?
check on her when she is sick. ?
hold her head when her head is paining.
offer her water.?
offer some medicine.?
kiss her cheeks. ?
tell her she's loved. ?
take care of her health.?
run your fingers through her hair. ?
put your head on her shoulder.?
kiss her neck. ?
give her soft kisses. ?
?
ask her about her dog. ?
was work tiring? ?
how is the family doing? ?
tell her what color dress suits her. hug her often. ?
remember the beating of her heart against your own chest. ?

look at her eyes. ?

look into her dark brown swirls of chocolate therein.?

?

tickle her. ?

tickle her till she squirming and giggling. ?

remember the warmth of her body on your hands. ?

listen to her.?

pay attention to every word that she is saying. ?

remember the look on her face when she tells you she loves you. ?

remember when you said it back. ?

tell her that you miss her. ?

remember all the ache you felt in her absence. ?

tell her to not bite her nails cause of the anxiety she has. ?

?

drop her texts on a rough day.?

send her your pictures. ?

remember the sound of her voice when she says your name. ?

capture her laugh. ?

say sorry to her when you should.

i appreciate it when she says thank you.?

readout novels to her before bed. ?

love her when she's grumpy. ?

stay over the phone when she is angry. ?

stay till she's calm down. ?

then stay some more.?

tell her that everything gonna fine.?

make things okay.
make things good.
?

love her like the world's gonna end tomorrow. ?
love her with the last bits of softness in your heart. ?
be kind to her. ?
love her calmly. ?
love her now. ?
love her like it's all you have ever known.?

# 49. Day '49'

love him hard. reach out for his hand when you're sitting in his passenger seat. entangle your fingers with his. kiss his cheeks. look at his face. watch how the corners of his mouth lift up when he smiles. watch some more. picture it in your mind. laugh at his silly jokes. laugh with him. remember his scent. go back to it when he's not around and you're missing him to the core. check on him when he's sick. hold his head when he's puking. offer him water. give some gum. kiss his cheeks.

tell him he's loved. in sickness and in health. run your fingers through his hair. run them just because. put your head on his shoulder. kiss his neck. give him soft kisses. remember how his skin feels against your lips.

ask him about his pet. was work tiring? how is dad? tell him what colors suit him. cuddle him. break into him. give comfortable hugs. remember the pulse of his heart against your own chest. look into his eyes. look at the brown swirls of chocolate therein. tickle him. tickle him till he's trembling and chuckling.

remember the zeal of his body on your hands. listen to him. pay attention to every word. remember the shape of his mouth when he tells you he loves you. remember the look on his face when you say you love him back. tell him you miss him. remember all the pain you've felt in his absence. and tell him. cut back his nails when he's too lazy to. kiss him. remember their pattern on his skin. leave him normal texts on a rough day. send him pictures. remember the sound of his voice when he says your name. memorize his laugh. say sorry to him when you should. i appreciate it when he says thank you. and, please. readout stories to him before bed. love him when he's grumpy. stay over the phone when he's angry. stay till he's calmed down. then stay some more. tell him everything will be okay. make things okay. make them good. love him like the world's ending tomorrow. love him with the last bits of softness in your heart. be kind to him. be warm. love him fearlessly. love him right now. love him like it's all you've ever known.

# 50. Day '50'

confess to her why you think you're in love with her. grab her up and throw her softly on the bed, tickle her till she begs you to stop and collect all the punches she throws at you to stop tickling. record her laugh and save it in your heart too. take her hand and give a warm kiss. just hold her hand and rest your head on her shoulder. let her play with your curly hairs. let her bite your ears and give you some kisses on the cheeks. just hold her hand.

go to your roof garden and pick some daisies and give to her take a handful of daisies and grace her hairs with them. take some pictures and give her a flying kiss because you found her really beautiful.

tell her to get dress because you planned something. take her to her's favorite momo shop. call your best friends and introduce her to them. talk to her and give a little bit extra attention to everything she says. look into her eyes and pass a smile to her.

go out for a walk with her. talk about her childhood memories and everything she tells you about her family. pay attention to her when she tries to tell about her first break-up and tear roll down through her eyes. wipe off her tears and give her a glass of water. tell her that it's okay. tuck her hair behind her ear and give her a forehead kiss. tell her that everything is gonna be just fine.

sit in the other room and start calling her with some cheesy nicknames. tell her about the articles you read which gave you a shock. ask her opinion about that. write poems and songs for her. take a guitar and sing no matter how you suck at singing your beautiful lyrics. cook dinner together and eat every bite she offers you with her hand no matter how full is your stomach. do dishes together and sing her some old romantic songs.

go to bed and rest your head on her lap. let her give you a head massage. enjoy the silence you share with her and enjoy the beautiful night. cuddle her and give her some kisses and sleep.

# 51. Day '51'

i am over you, i swear i am over you. when i wake up it's not your thought that crosses my mind. i wake up, have my tea and scroll through the newsfeed. i am glad that I dared to unfollow you on social media so that your pictures with your new partner do not show up. i am happy.

last night, i went out with my friends for dinner after a long time. i was no more than just happy. i got home back, changed into my usual clothes shorts, and tees then started scrolling through the stories updates on instagram. suddenly, i stopped and saw your pic on your friend's story. what was it that hit me? nostalgia? pain? numbness? i don't know.

i tried sleeping. but all I did was just toss and turn myself on my bed, made my pillows wet, and wonder about possibilities. what would if you showed up? would I stay able to move on? would i able to look straight into your eyes and say, "you're not the only one i want?" i don't know i have no answers.

"what is this about love?"

why do people leave, only to come back and make you realise how they never left in the first place?

# 52. Day '52'

to the person who will love him next,

i know you will think that he is not very expressive when it comes to love. even though he will say "i love you" a hundred times in a day. all you need to learn to appreciate it. sometimes it's "you had food?" other times it, "drop me a text when you'll reach home", or "you can have the last slice or spoon of food" or just two arms cuddling you tighter. just understand all the little things before it's too late.

his calmness may not give you a clue that he loves conversation. but, he will talk about the problems that millennials facing or some geopolitical decisions that India took. maybe he will confuse between two dresses when it comes to choosing one but don't freak out because he thinks that you look beautiful in both. even though he is not good with dresses but he will always find perfect earrings and footwear for them. he hangs back when you tell him that your favorite color is black not because he doesn't want to say anything he pauses because he wanted to know why black is your favorite color. talk to him and don't think that he is not paying attention to your talks he always does it's just he never shows.

memorize, that you're not the first person whose hands he is going to hold or whose cheeks he is gonna pull or forehead he is gonna kiss. that doesn't mean he is doing that same thing he is done before because you're not unique to him, or because he doesn't make an effort to distinguish between past and present partners. but that's how does distinguish between the person his heart belongs to right now and everyone else in the world. people realise it a little when it was too late but you don't make this mistake.

# 53. Day '53'

one day you gonna meet a girl who'll make you forget that you were ever shattered or that you are incomplete.

she will notice the way you take care of every little thing.

she will find the child behind the man you always hide.

she will notice the way you look at the moon and she will wanna look at you the same way.

she will understand the reason behind your silence when you are not fine.

she will remember the way you talk when you're drunk.

she will know how confused and adamant you get when you're overworked, and she will still want to love you, including the way you look in your awful photos, in every new haircut you get because of the barber's mistake, the way you laugh and grunt in between, the way you become so sophisticated when it comes to eating, the scars on your body, and she will still choose to love you enormously and she will still be proud of you because she is not the one who shattered you.

she will never ask you to talk more and silently enjoy your silence.

she might get angry at times but she will make sure that you're fine.

she will not gonna ask you to change the way you look or to wear better clothes, but she will help you with shopping. she will never break your heart and she will never leave your hand when you hold.

instead of taking you to some fancy dates, she will want you to just make her a cup of tea when she comes late from work and had a tiring day and just read her a book till she dozes off and be there for her, that is the person you deserve. until then don't let anyone treat you badly.

# 54. Day '54'

here you are once again, debating whether or not you should respond to a call from someone. your heart tells you yes, go help that someone, in a world where it seems that people like you are nothing more than "snowflakes" and "weaklings." your mind reminds you of all the times when you were in the exact same situation and didn't receive a single thing and all the times when your cries for help were ignored by people hardened by our world. respond to that person. say yes, even if you will never see them when you need them most.

it's hard to care so much in a world that seems to have stopped caring. you're called naive when you once again help someone whom everyone else has refused. you're called fake when you try your hardest to include everyone in your daily life and try to make everyone's day better. you seem pushy when you try everything you can to see someone who isn't smiling, smile. you seem awkward and weird when you want to sit down and talk to someone who isn't having a good day.

it's hard to stay strong. it's hard to keep caring when the world encourages you to create your own selfish cocoon in which your needs will always dominate those of others. the world screams at you: "it's a selfish world, and the selfish succeed."

don't listen. don't let the picture that a small portion of the world has covered up your entire exhibit. don't stop caring, even when you feel that it really is all for nothing and your deeds are forgotten (trust me it is the exact opposite). don't stop, because when you get to where you are going, you will look back on all the times your heart told you to blindly care and realize that those were the most fulfilling moments of your life. you will have experiences that left you feeling better not only after a long day but also after a long and care-filled life.

to the people who care way too much, your light is what the world needs right now more than ever, and that light is more valuable than any material object on this earth.

always care, because people won't remember what you said, or what you did, but they will never forget the way you made them feel.

# 55. Day '55'

and then I found out how to laugh when you are around me. no, not the smile I wore on my face to trick the world into imagining that I was happy. i am talking about the times when I stared at you struggling with a bowl of noodles from across the table and you'd look up at me with too much hanging from your mouth and I swear, I swear I wanted to kiss you in front of all those people, noodles and all and tell you the truth. the truth?
i have never been happier with anyone. i have never been more in love with anything in this world as I have loved the brown of your eyes, the cute nose that you think is big and weird, the chubby cheeks, or the pimples you were so embarrassed about. i have never felt so alive. i have never wanted something to work out so badly, desperately.

# 56. Day '56'

dear voices in my head,

as silly as it might be to be writing to the one thing that controls all my thoughts and emotions, I just wanted to express these thoughts and emotions out loud because you have been asking me to write this for months.

it's kinda hard living with you I'm not going to lie; you are not the easiest to understand. i mean, I appreciate how thoughtful and understanding you are. you care and that's important. people recognise how prudent we are; they know that we are trustworthy and accountable. but don't you ever get tired of always trying to please — always thinking about what others might say or do? I know I'm sure tired, exhausted even. maybe it's time to take a break and relax; I'm sure that we both would sustain from a little downtime.

really what I want to be writing to you about is all the outrageous thing that seems to throw off you. i know that change brings more change, but I wish that you could be a little more satisfied with how good things have been going. instead, you seem to be getting caught up in everything hard or irritating. you have to remember that friends are fluid at the moment — every relationship is new and different and not getting success doesn't mean you have to stop trying for another time.

please be kind to yourself, please be patient and, most of all,
please love yourself.

love,

me.

# 57. Day '57'

dear you,

so how do you do it?

get over something that meant the world to you?

you're sitting on a milestone beside a dark highway. having a smoke and a cup of tea. you have traveled far from home, cutting through traffic on your own. you are astounded, you made it this far cause this is your first drive alone. your head feels absolutely blank, with the cold breeze and the smell from a faraway rain reminding you of a place you once loved. but other than that, it's a mixed feeling of relief and calm. you're scared. you are scared that you feel okay, that after so long, you're actually present somewhere else.

is it okay to be okay when you have no reason to be okay?

you need to understand something. your time here is very very restricted. it's uncertain. you need to understand that it's okay to go after the one you have loved. but only to a certain point. a bit more than halfway. you need to understand that it's okay to outgrown things that meant the world to you.

it is okay to let go when all you had ever wanted was to hold on to that person cause they had promised you forever. it's okay to let yourself forget them slowly cause you will never actually forget them, only the impact they have on you will fade away with time. it's okay to be okay when you have every reason not to.

get up. what you had will always be a part of you. but you're so much more than that just someone's someone. and not knowing who you are is the best part about being in love with life.

# 58. Day '58'

In the space between your words, the silence sits like punctuations. i stare back at you as you look away, and the lights of the traffic signal behind us turn green from red. when you look back at me, it reflects in your eyes, your smile. you always smile when you catch me staring at you. it's time for us to go home, you say. it's getting late. your mother gets worried. i take the last drag from my cigarette and pick up my phone to book a cab. you stare back at the people crossing the street, the cars passing by, the chai wala making rounds...
"do you miss her ?" you ask me...
"no, I don't." i look away, shrug...
"stop lying. you don't have to be such a hardass all the time. at least not around me.
"i feel rattled. it's somewhat horrifying that you can see through me like I'm made of glass when nobody else could...
"hey. stop trying to fight it. you loved her, parts of you still do. if it disappeared just like that overnight, it wasn't loved to begin with right?"
then you do that thing you do, you space out for a second... staring at everything yet nothing and for a second...
i get a glimpse of her sitting beside me, staring at the setting sun. it breaks me, rips my lungs out from the inside. but then it settles, at the bottom of my chest like sand underwater. I

don't fight it anymore, let it take over me, wash over me... and then disperse, like smoke across a blue sky...
"let's go home dumbass. you have a lot of packing to do. leaving is hard work."
you get up and light a cigarette.
hard work.
yes.
necessary?
yes.

# 59. Day '59'

do you know what is beautiful?

your hair, when a gentle wind blows and you somehow manage to put your tresses behind your ear with your forefinger, which still looks the prettiest without any piece of jewelry.

your cheeks, in the winter mornings which made the rose feel pale with the pink color which perfectly shined on the snow-white skin of yours.

your brown eyes, which still look the prettiest without applying any texture on, the ones which never fail to fascinate me, a pair of two crystalline yet expressive eyes.

your fingers, when they get perfectly locked within mine and crushing of your soft hand against my palm which still manages to give me goosebumps.

your naive morning face, wearing nothing on it but your smile and a pair of dimples making it look more charming.

you, when you are with me.

# 60. Day '60'

listen, the world is an awful place.

there's no scruple about it.

but you're worth more than what it will cost you.

"look closer"

just a glimpse, she's just a face in the mob.

just a glimpse, she's just another casual person.

just a glimpse, she's just "that girl"

but if you were to look closer, just a little, you would see something new.

like the smoothness of her hair, or her new hairstyle.

look a bit more closer, notice her dress matches her eyes.

note the way she walks when she's determined.

look even closer, notice the shining sparkle in her eyes, and how the sound of her laughter quickly pulls you up after a wild day.

now close your eyes.

feel the beat of her heart, and how it matches yours.

# 61. Day '61'

it never occurred to me that i love you. not in the typical romantic way in movies when they look into each other's eyes, wrap their arms in an embrace, and kiss in the rain. nothing like that.

it was always the little things that made me fall in love with you. the first small walk we took. the home-cooked chocolates that bring for me. the acts of the understanding you'd show when i'm feeling down. the moments where we'd laugh because of a stupid lame joke. the times we spent together made me smile.

the little things, add up every day and makes a whole heart last a lifetime. it's a beautiful yet terrifying thing when knowing that you're a part of me. what if you were gone, i'd feel incomplete without you. what do you think? is this true?

sometimes i think i'll lose you too. if i'm burdening you with the pain i feel, the weight of my deep sadness on your shoulders, and the hours of agonizing silence where i left words unspoken. the words 'you are stupid, but i love you, and i'm always here for you.'

it's hard to validate our feelings. when oftentimes, we both couldn't even begin to explain why they motivated us to do certain things for each other. but when i closed my eyes before falling asleep, i could feel the warmth beating in my chest knowing that having you in my life makes me feel like the luckiest person in the world.

i still carry the seasons of our love every day. sometimes it's an airy summer day, and sometimes it's a dark winter under blankets of snow. it changes, and it goes, with all the highs and the lows, it is still loved that grows.

i love you more than you'll ever know in this lifetime, and it will go on even when my heart flatlines.

there are no more words left to write that could even begin to explain who i love, why love, what i love, where love, and how i love.

i love you in every universe.

# 62. Day '62'

there was this girl i met on the internet.

she was pretty, was fascinated by philosophy, and keeps coming up with these strange philosophical solutions for everything. was really smart too. had a lovely pug. we chatted for a few days. passed to night long phonecalls. before long, we were going to sleep post wishing each other good morning. we met after few months. i saw her from a distance as she waited for me at this bus stop. a little fidgety. nothing like your eased up grace. straight brown hair. white t-shirt. blue denim. torn black jeans. white sneakers. she's prettier than you, but you were taller. we exchanged a hug, she smelled of lavender and yardley. quite different of you.

after we find a table for two. we ordered a matcha latte and my favorite swiss choco-chip pancakes at you-know-that eatery well. i wiped a speck away from the edge of her lips as i listened to her talking ceaselessly about her ex, although i had by then memorised that story. but i was attentive because nowadays people barely do... or was it because i didn't wanna talk about you? she giggles a lot, you know. she looks adorable when she does that. but her eyes are always sad. like they hold a lot of pain. we roamed around the city all day, went for fuss ball. i had to teach her, recalling all the times you knock me in every game. after evening, we sat at a park bench by the lake as evening settled in. she kept her head on my shoulder and hummed a line of elvis presley. i could smell the conditioner in her hair. i asked her something, she looked up at me. i could see the flicker of hope and the longing to be held screaming out from behind those beautiful dark hazel eyes. she gently kept her fingers on my cheeks. as our lips met, i felt something tearing my heart to bits. i flinched...and she understood and pulled herself back.

things have been awkward ever since. it's been days, we haven't spoken since i dropped her home. i apologised. she told me it's totally okay...

but you know, it's not okay.

it's not because the whole time we were together, there was a continuous analogy in my mind between you and her..

...it wasn't okay because i couldn't make myself tell her that the last person i kissed was you and somehow i didn't want to change that. i couldn't tell her that i was thinking up things, that when she talked about her favourite tv show, i kept ticking off the ones i knew you had been watching, or when she said she loved carrot cheesecake, i inescapably remembered the time we were stuck in your favorite cafe for an hour just to have that.

i couldn't tell her that my mind needs fixing, or how i still think of you the way a little one thinks of his first memory. like the first sensation of touch, i can recall was the tip of my fingers leaving goosebumps on your skin, like the first breath i ever took was your smile against my lips as we kissed, like the first thing i ever saw was the sun melting into your eyes as it had finally found a home in mine.

tell me i forgot you... and i'll show you how the earth never forgets the smell of rain, or the sky the sound of wings.

but i've been chasing your mirage for so long i lost track of time. and lately, i've been letting you slip away from the corners of my mind.

and one of these days, i'll see her again... and this time, maybe i'll make the first step, kiss her till we're out of breath. i won't flinch because it's been so long i've forgotten what it feels like. probably this time, i'll look at her and not see you... and when she'll stop to take a picture in the middle of a packed street, staring up at the sundown, i'll remember the way she sparkles when she smiles... and promise to myself to make her smile like that for the rest of her life. i will take my time to know her, what makes her the happiest, what keeps her up at night. i'll not rush things like you and me, i will try to be her best friend first, laugh with her, hold her when she cries. and it's okay if we don't say the words till we feel it's safe to say so. maybe we won't work out, but i'm ready to take my chances.

and maybe, months later, on a cold winter saturday night. i'll tell her about you.

do i miss you? sometimes, i do.

but more than that, i miss who i was before you left.

i miss being holding on to life.

# 63. Day '63'

"to be in love is so beautiful, right?" he whispered into her ear on that wintry night. we were sitting and gazing at the stars. "what else do you think they say you never lived if you never loved?" she whispered.

he gazes at her with those mellow eyes. she looks back. those eyes, intense and radiant she could go to the war for them. there was something so different than all she had gaped into her entire life. they were filled with love and zeal and calmness all at the same time. as if it was the clam before and after the storm and the storm itself, all at once. as if she was looking at the thing she was chasing her whole life. and it convinced her that she was a clod. love found her when she stopped believing it to come.

love made her dance in the moonlight under the beautiful starry night, kissed her with those radiant lips. love always kept murmuring in her ears, all that it was fond of.

so, he moves closer towards her and takes her hand and points it to the sky, and says, "do you see that?" that's the north star. the brightest one. and she never looks at the star. she was looking at him and beholds a sky filled with stars. that can blind her with its brightness. and its darkness could embrace her each night when she grows insecure about everything. all at once.

and he looks at her looking at him and she looks away "stop staring at me! haven't you ever seen a sky brighter than me?!" "no, not once," she murmured.

we lie there for a while. and the first ray of sun peers through the clouds as if it is trying to see her falls in love for the first time.

and she asks him,

"so, what do we do now that we've loved?!"

"we leave."

# 64. Day '64'

there is something more addictive about sleeplessness that people, who are not used to it, won't understand. the world shifts into a strange place when nobody is looking. it's 1:00 AM and i am standing on the terrace of my building in a far-off city, full of smiling strangers. the road outside is full of traffic even at this hour. there are people too, teenagers going home from clubs playing pretentious music in their luxurious cars. this city never dozes off, just like me.

one blind beggar is standing on the edge of the road, taping his bowl on the sidewalk. he wants to pass over the road. but he was unable to do it cause of flashing cars at breakneck speed every five seconds. i am thinking of going down there and lending him a hand.

i haven't been competent to put down anything since i got here. maybe it's just because of a sudden change of surroundings that has left me overwhelmed or maybe i have lost myself in the mansions and the brightening light around me. i have always had big dreams. bigger ambitious. but deep inside me, i am still that person who comes from another city, scribbling on his notebook with his little doggie.

somewhere deep inside, i am a 24-year-old guy, who is awfully sensible now about life who's too ashamed to admit that he misses his mom as a ten-year-old does. i have left so much behind, ripped out every thread that is connected me with my home, left so many goodbyes unsaid, so many chapters unfinished. it's strange how i seem to have lost every memory i had of who i used to be, who i loved, what i lost. i can't seem to remember anything ..... and it terrifies me.

a cab just pulled up at the gate of my street and a girl stumbled out. she can't even walk straight through all the booze in her. i hope she gets home safe. the blind beggar found an exit and crossed the road on his own.

i should too.

# 65. Day '65'

sometimes it's okay to be alone. being alone allows you to step away from the rush and fuss of life. between schools, colleges, internships, jobs, activities, and your social life, it's important to take a break for yourself. it doesn't matter what you do, whether it's reading, watching, cooking, dancing like no one is watching you, or listening to your favorite music on repeat mode and enjoy your own presence, whatever you're doing is completely credible.

try to step out of your comfort zone, and make an effort to do something new by yourself. in the past months, i have joined one photography class. every couple of days, i'd showed up to the class, and made friends with people who had been doing photography for years, and who were much older than me. it was intimidating at first because they were a lot better, but they made me better and corrected my (often incorrect) technique.

there was a time when didn't always talk to people when was in my class. there were the days when i would just focus on concepts and details of photography. i was clicking so many pictures as i could, and let go of whatever was bothering me. find things that make you calm and not think about the stress of maintaining a 'perfect' life. that's when you'll find out what you truly enjoy, not what you think you enjoy because of the people around you, or because of irrelevant influence.

you know there is one quote of oscar wilde that, "you need to know how to be alone and not be defined by another person." the moment you stop comparing yourself to others (whether through looks, career, or achievements), you become the best possible version of yourself.

you know just cause you're alone, doesn't mean that you're lonely. it's better to be alone than surrounded by the wrong people. another great thing that being alone has taught me is how to find friends that you know you can trust and will get along with. it taught me how to sit back and observe others, to listen to their stories, and to be patient.

if you're lonely, don't be scared of reach out to people, and surrounded by friends who will support you, cause they exist.

# 66. Day '66'

loving, loving can hurt sometimes.

yes, he put down it right.

love is something that is not just an emotion it's something more than that.

people are not afraid of falling in love, at first sight. they are afraid of getting hurt after falling in love. they are afraid of their first heartbreak after falling in love.

love is something that people go awry about but it's not like that. love is not about liking someone, not by their looks and body. it's like falling in love with its heart. you have to accept the flaws and all the scars.

reality should be loved not what we make you see. in love, you should love the shortcomings, not perfection. well everybody falls in love with somebody, someday or another day. sometimes it's not unavoidable that what you think it actually loves. i fell in love with the new people i meet every day. i observe them, admire them a accept their flaws. i learn while love.

you can love someone with or without any intention. loving someone deeply hurts cause it's not meant to be perfect. after all, they might not think the way you think about them. "it's, not your fault." it's for every failed lover.

don't love someone cause he or she loves you. don't love someone abruptly just causes they are good to you. don't love just cause you to find them cute, alluring, beautiful, or handsome. don't love someone just cause looks have become fundamental. don't love someone just cause you wanna it's time to get over your past.

love someone when you think you're discovering and evolving into a better person. love without learning is indented. love someone when you think that it's time for you to give the respect that they deserve when you see that they have always put you up in any drowning dilemmas. love someone when you truly start loving yourself. there is no giving love without furnishing that love to yourself first. don't let it became your deficiency. don't let it start influencing you and you stop thinking about yourself. if you're not learning and becoming better while you love then you are not "loving".

# 67. Day '67'

it's been years since i have re-read our old conversations. it took me an hour to scroll down to the beginning of our chats. when the words are reluctant, calculated. back when we were two strangers who had yet to find out each other, yet to become friends, yet to fall in love.

last night i passed by your building, taking a stroll down the streets where we used to take those small walks, that park in front of your building where we used to sit in the evening gossiping about some random things. i sat there for a couple of minutes just to see that it weaken me like it used to.

it didn't.

it's been a long time since we stopped calling each other in the middle of the night, toured meaningless talks with strangers to pass the time. when my strength to never call you again was deteriorating every minute i spent huddled up in the bed unable to sleep, missing you. i longed to hear your voice one last time hoping that would help me to sleep and yet i suppressed every thought of you. i couldn't depend on you to put me off to sleep like you used to.

it's been more than a year since we have given up on each other... and i think i am doing better. but, what i would not do scroll us back to the beginning of our conversation, just to start our conversation again. start over again, with you.

# 68. Day '68'

okay, lemme tell you
about her.
what do i name her?
a riddle. a mystery.
gorgeous confusion to me.
a puzzle i couldn't crack
a fairytale from my childhood
i sometimes rule out to believe.
you see...
i glanced as the whole world
fell in love with her in front of my eyes,
every day, all around me.
like she wasn't human like she was made
of stardust mixed in the hurricane...
with freckles of compassion,
a pinch of decent grace that shone through her skin as if her
bones were fluorescent, home to fireflies with neon wings.
it wasn't about how beautiful she was it was how she saw
beauty in every little thing
and she wore her flaws with the same comfort as her black hair
let down, in waves, on a rainy sunday.
you see, she was rare.
i could see it

in her eyes...
and I bet she knew that she had my heart...
i bet she knew because every time
she smiled at me from across the room,
i felt my heart miss a few beats.
and me?
i was folly in love with her
not being able to figure out if she was blind or brave... or
completely silly
she had the world at her feet.
and still
she chose to fall in love
with me.

# 69. Day '69'

you don't need to rush for love.

you will know when the true one will come.

you will see them staring and glowing at you like you're the happiest thing that happened to them.

every time they will hold your hand, you'll feel the same warmth, the same feeling, and the same rate of beats increasing every second.

you will feel the safest having their arms around you and just like the cologne they left on your body, they'll stay in your life.

they will know your darkest insecurities, your fears and will help you overcome them, together.

they will make you love yourself a little more than before and you'll know things about you, you were unaware of.

they'll be happy by just having you around them and will do any craziest thing just to see you smile, one more time.

you deserve such pure, unconditional love and it'll be waiting for you on your journey. grab it.

you don't need to rush for love. you'll just know when the right one will come.

# 70. Day '70'

there is this girl i know who tends to stay up all night listening
to music that reminisces her of some specific situations.
the one who suppresses her anxiety, grief, suffering, and cracks
under her beautiful fake smile and giggles.
the one who implores things will work out just for one time
and she will be assuaged.
the one who moans and cries in her pillow because the rest of
the world goes awry to listen.
the one who has it arduous but doesn't let anyone know that.
the one who has many enigmas but never lets out.
the one who stays up wondering if someone will ever notice.
the one who does not always gain a victory.
the one who takes life the way it gets to.
the one who will love all the hearts.
there is this girl I know and it's you.

# 71. Day '71'

as she enters the grocery store, she could listen to people starts whispering.

"yaa, it's her."

"she is surely a weirdo"

"i don't know how do they do it?"

"maybe the steel harms? or would it be iron? or is it like the terminator one?"

men and women, laughing, making fun, and laughing at her. wanda has had enough.

she stops walking and stands still for a few seconds. suddenly all the murmuring ends.

she veers around back to face her nitpicker, her bullies, her insecurities, all at once and then starts saying out loud.

"what makes you all think that only your way of love is the right way? why can't mine be regarded natural? just because you people cannot understand it? or is it because you all, in your stupid jagged thin mean mind deemed it wrong?"

there was pin-drop silence in the grocery store.

wanda could feel tears filling up her eyes and her voice trembling.

she begins again.

"so many of you here have had failed relationships, marriages that ended up in a 'divorce.

so many of you, with partners who cheated on you, with whom you cheated on, and yet, you people dare to sit and make fun of me?

so how does it make a fuss? do you think my husband is incapable to express emotions?

well, he can. probably more than anyone among you.

why does, some part of my life, affect yours's so much?

wiping the tears that rolled down her cheeks, she asks aloud, "why does it bother you, that my husband is not a human, but a synthezoid ?"

# 72. Day '72'

dear i,

i know how you may be feeling and we know it is hard. you may find yourself constantly craving the love and affection that was present in a past relationship after experiencing something so great, how is it even possible to live without it? when you put your trust in someone and they let you down, you may find yourself searching for that "next one" to fill the void. this habit isn't just mentally and physically exhausting, but it can also eradicate every ounce of self-confidence that you have.

it's easy to feel alone sometimes. after all, when you find yourself hours away from home, buried in work and other responsibilities, life can be extremely stressful. you might feel a desperate need for "someone" who can bring you an origin of solace that seems to be lacking in your life. still, you have to believe in the power of fate.

in all things of life especially love anything you have to urge is probably not truly meant to be. do not place your emotional well-being into someone who, deep down, you know isn't right for you. more importantly, don't fool yourself into settling for less than you deserve in moments of vulnerability. you don't have to ignite a new flame to heal the burn of an old flame. time is the best medicine and it makes you so much stronger in the end.

the first step in loving someone else is wholeheartedly loving yourself. never encourage yourself that the reason why you're single is because you're not good enough for someone. everybody has a plan maybe yours is just taking a little longer to be put into action. once you start taking on all the great things in your life, you will surely be on the road to true happiness. as your independence grows, your confidence will grow right along with it. after all, the best relationship you can have is the one you have with yourself.

you have a lifetime ahead of you and you will hit upon many different people along the way. not just in connections, but in life as a whole, the best things happen when you least expect them. good things come to those who wait and you deserve the best!

yours,

A.!

# 73. Day '73'

he looks like a fancy individual, but only I know that he doesn't like going to costly restaurants for dates. not that he's not romantic but he inclines toward watching sunsets on the beaches, holding me closer to him. his hugs so safe, I feel like I'm being put inside his chest. may god bless his sweatshirts

he dances awful like a ten-year-old but has never refused dancing with me. his legs would never sync with the song but he'd still manage to impress me. it's not always about the outcome, but the efforts. the slow dances where he'd hold me by my waist, gripping fingers and the prolonged stares at each other felt like I was living ed's 'thinking out loud'. "maybe we found love right where we ar

listening to our favorite playlist every night, to finishing off each others' sentences, we've reached a long way. i often fall asleep while babbling to him on the phone and wake up to his voice notes. i never ask forgiveness for fall asleep. he never complained about it onc

he likes gazing at the night sky like some hopeless old-school romantic. he loves all the levels of the moon equally. his eyes shine when he looks at them. and trust me, i've noticed the same glimmer in his eyes when he talks to me, smiling, keeping gentle eye contac he loves evenings because of sunsets. he loves capturing the sun meeting the blue somewhere near the horizon and exclaiming "what a beauty!" you know, the way he describes the shades of red, yellow, and orange, really thought sunsets were the ones he's in love with until i flunked to find even a single picture of a sunset on his phone. it was all m

so tell me, how many songs, slow dances, forehead kisses, sunsets, prolonged stares, late-night calls does it take to confirm that this is the 'love' thing

now, when we're sitting on the seaside holding hands and him kissing me on my forehead and on my cheeks, i'm counting. it's 104 songs till date. how many more, can you tell?y?e.t.e.e"._e likes more, can you tell?

# 74. Day '74'

maybe you lost someone you never expected you would lose.

maybe you lost yourself, that's even worse.

when you have bad days that just won't let up.

i hope you just look into the mirror and remind yourself of what you are and what you're not.

you're not your mistake.

you're not damaged goods or muddy from your failed explorations.

you're not the opinion of someone who doesn't know you.

you're the product of the lesson you've learned.

you're wise because you went through something terrible.

and you're the person who survived a bunch of rainstorms and kept walking.

i now believe that pain makes you stronger.

and i believe that walking through a bunch of rainstorms gets you clean.

# 75. Day '75'

to the love I thought would last forever,

i've heard it said that you only find that one great love once in your lifetime. an emotional and full love that makes you question how you went so long without that person in your life. a love that feels safe, a love that feels right, an exhilarating love, and a love that changes you in a way that you thought was never possible - a love that makes you a better person.

the thought of losing that love at all is unimaginable, unthinkable, and yet the reality is that sometimes love does not work out in your favor - even if you believe that person could be the one. i thought I had finally found that kind of love.

after sharing a year of laughs, singing at the top of our lungs on our little road trips, calling each other on the phone just to hear the other's voice, and the many other amazing memories we shared that I will never forget, we parted ways for what you thought was for the best. and maybe you were right, but I still can't help but wish it could have been different.

i may miss the person I fell in love with, the person I called my best friend, but like most things in life, I have to accept the fact that there is nothing I can do to change the past. so I've distanced myself; I've kept myself busy with college and work, and though I wouldn't say I've been great, I am okay and I will get through it.

life still goes on - even if life's once vibrant colors have dimmed and the days taste more bitter than sweet, things will get better with each day. You will always hold a special place in my heart, and who knows what the future holds, maybe someday things will change but for now, I will take care of myself and only hope for the best.

www.ingramcontent.com/pod-product-compliance
Lightning Source LLC
Chambersburg PA
CBHW021214130726
47988CB00002B/659